The Complete Keto Crock Pot Cookbook

Super-Tasty Low Fat Recipes To Keep Yourself Fit.
Lose Weight Fast And Get Lean In A Few Steps
With Amazing And Foolproof Recipes

Clara Smith

Table of Contents

Introduction

The crockpot has long been a favorite kitchen implement for the 'set-it-and-forget-it' meal. It's a wonderful invention by whoever thought it up, and it has saved many a few dollars on electricity by not needing to keep the stove and oven on for extended hours and all day. So, what really is a crockpot?

A crockpot is also called a slow cooker or a casserole crockpot. These nicknames refer to the same kitchen appliance, and it is one of the most used reheating methods today. It is basically a cooker with a glazed ceramic bowl that has a tight sealing lid. It is because of the liquid that will go in with the food. The crockpot is then plugged into an electrical socket in the kitchen for it to work.

The crockpot slow cooking method involves basically depositing the ingredients you desire to cook into the crockpot bowl (usually by stirring it with a wooden spoon or a ladle), adding the liquid of choice, cooking it for a few hours until it's done. These used to be the standard cooking methods in kitchens, and they have stayed the same with the invention of the crockpot. Nowadays, most crockpots have interiors thermostatically controlled to ensure that it's set at the right temperature during the cooking process to not over-cook your meals.

The best in crockpot slow cooking is finding that low and slow recipe. Recipes that are low in time length are usually very low in steps, and not much work is involved. It usually leads to the much sought after 'set it and forget it' kind of meal. Imagine not having to watch your meals cook slowly as you work on other tasks; you can avoid the temptation of peeking or checking on it too often and not having to worry about burning or crusting on the sides of your crockpot. When cooking at low heat, you don't have to worry about your meal exploding all over the kitchen or all the grease falling out and sticking to the bottom of your crock.

The best use of crockpot slow cooking is the convenience of the food, especially during holidays and parties. You can set the crockpot down on the table, and everyone can serve themselves. It is an excellent and great way to spend time with your guests and treat them well. There is nothing cheesier than eating the same dish fondue style. You get to enjoy slow cooking hotdogs for hours and hours without little ones surreptitiously taking off the top and poaching them in the pool of oil sitting beside the dish.

A crockpot is a very good way to use leftovers for a delicious meal. If you cook a large meal regularly and you have leftovers, put them in a crockpot with a liquid and let it cook. It will double the amount of food leftover or fed to the cat at the end of the week.

CHAPTER 1:

Breakfast

1.   Cauliflower Breakfast Casserole

Preparation time: 15 minutes

Cooking time: 0 hours

Servings: 5-7

Ingredients:

- 1 cup of shredded cheddar cheese

- 4 slices of low sodium, all natural turkey bacon, cooked and diced

- 1/2 small bell pepper, diced

- 1/2 small onion, diced

- Salt and pepper

- 1/2 head cauliflower

- 1/4 teaspoon pepper

- 1/2 teaspoon Himalayan salt

- 1/8 teaspoon dry mustard

- 2 tablespoons unsweetened almond milk

- 4 large eggs

Directions:

1. Coat a crock pot with coconut oil or olive oil spray and set aside. Then mix together dry mustard, eggs, salt, almond milk and pepper in a large bowl.

2. Put around 1/3 of the cauliflower in the bottom of the crockpot and top with one third of the bell pepper and onion.

3. Season with pepper and salt, and top with one third of the cheese and one third of the bacon. Repeat the layers two more rounds.

4. At this point, pour the egg mixture over the layers of the ingredients in the crockpot. Cook until the eggs are set and browned at the top, for about 5-7 hours or so. Serve and enjoy.

Nutrition:

Calories 324.5

Fat 22.5g

Carbs 7.5g

Protein 22.6g

2.   Simple Cauliflower Breakfast

Preparation time: 15 minutesCooking time: 3 hours & 8 minutes

Servings: 4

Ingredients:

- 4 oz. Cheddar cheese

- 1/8 teaspoon salt

- 3 eggs

- 1/2 leek, cut into quarter inch half-moon slices

- 6 cooked sausage links, cut into quarter inch rounds

- 2 1/2 oz. cremini mushrooms, finely diced

- 1/8 teaspoon salt

- 5 oz. cauliflower florets

Directions:

1. Grease a crockpot with cooking spray and set aside. Meanwhile add pieces of the cauliflower to a heat-safe bowl along with salt.

2. Add water to the bowl and fill it to entirely cover the cauliflower, and put it in the microwave to cook for about 8 minutes.

3. As it cooks, be preparing the leeks, sausage and mushrooms. Then drain off the liquid from the half cooked cauliflower and add it to the crockpot.

4. Evenly distribute the sausage and mushrooms pieces on the cauliflower and set aside. Now whisk together salt and eggs in a bowl and carefully stir in cleaned leeks. Slowly stir in half of the cheese and reserve the other half.

5. Then pour the egg mixture uniformly over the cauliflower pieces, sausage and the mushrooms. Cover the ingredients and cook on high for about 2 to 3 hours, or until the eggs puff up.

6. At this point, sprinkle the rest of the cheese over the top and allow it to melt. Then slice the casserole and enjoy. Season the dish with salt and pepper if you like.

Nutrition: Calories 356.5 Fat 29.9g Carbs 4.5g Protein 18.9g

3.   **Breakfast Meatloaf**

Preparation time: 15 minutes

Cooking time: 0 hours

Servings: 4

Ingredients:

- 1/2 teaspoon sea salt

- 1/2 teaspoon paprika

- 1/2 teaspoon black pepper

- 1 teaspoon dried thyme

- 1 teaspoon ground sage

- 1 teaspoon red pepper flakes

- 1 teaspoon dried oregano

- 1 teaspoon fennel seeds, ground

- 1/2 garlic powder

- 4 tablespoons almond flour

- 1 egg

- 1 lb. ground pork

- 1 cup diced onion

- 1/2 tablespoon coconut oil

Directions:

1. At medium-low heat, soften the onion in a tablespoon of oil until transparent. Then remove from heat and let cool. Add all the ingredients to a large bowl apart from the ground pork. Stir or whisk to blend.

2. Add in the softened onions and the ground pork to the bowl and combine the ingredients manually using your hands.

3. Then pick the meat mixture and put it in the center of the crockpot's insert. Shape it into a loaf and position it half an inch from the sides of the insert.

4. Once done, pat the top the loaf and close the crockpot's lid. Cook the meatloaf on low for 3 hours, or until the internal temperature is 150 degrees F.

5. Then let the meatloaf cool for up to 30 minutes after turning off the crockpot and removing the lid to make it easier to remove the meatloaf. Move to a separate dish.

6. You can serve immediately or keep it refrigerated overnight and serve for breakfast. To serve, simply reheat the slices at medium low heat for a minute or two.

Nutrition:

Calories 412.6

Fat 28.7g

Carbs 5.0g

Protein 32.5g

4.   **Breakfast Frittata**

Preparation time: 15 minutes

Cooking time: 2-3 hours

Servings: 3

Ingredients:

- 2/3 cups cook sausage, breakfast

- 1/2 teaspoon sea salt

- 1/4 teaspoons black pepper

- 4 individual beat eggs

- 2 tablespoons dice onion, red

- 3/4 cups dice bell pepper, red

- 3 ounce drain spinach, frozen

Directions:

1. Mix together spinach, sea salt, black pepper, eggs, red onions, sausage and red pepper in an oil-greased Crockpot.

2. Cover and cook for 2-3 hours on low or until set. In case you'd like to freeze the frittata, cool it for a moment then cut into equal-sized portions. Then divide it among 1 gallon freezer bags and keep it frozen until ready to serve.

Nutrition:

Calories 238

Carbs 3g

Fat 16g

Protein 20g

5.   Cheese and Mushroom Strata

Preparation time: 15 minutes Cooking time: 0 hours

Servings: 3 Ingredients:

- 1/8 teaspoon salt

- 1/2 tablespoon Dijon

- 1 tablespoon thyme, finely chopped

- 1 1/4 cups milk 4 eggs

- 1 cup grated gruyere cheese

- Keto friendly bread, cut into 1-inch pieces 2 1/2 thick slices

- 1/2 -227g package cremini mushrooms, sliced

- 1/2 tablespoon Olive oil

Directions:

1. Over medium-high heat, melt oil in a non-stick frying pan. Add in mushrooms and cook for about 5-6 minutes, or until the mushrooms are tender and their liquid evaporated.

2. Using a large piece of coil, line the bottoms and sides of a Crockpot. Lightly coat with oil. Cover the bottom with a third of the bread then scatter the mushrooms over the bread.

3. Sprinkle the mixture with a third of the cheese, and then add half of the remaining bread, and the rest of mushrooms and cheese. Add the remaining bread on top.

4. At this point, beat eggs with Dijon, thyme and milk in a large bowl. Pour the mixture over the bread and season with fresh pepper.

5. Carefully press down the bread to soak into the mixture and top with cheese. Cook on low for 8 hours. Once set, open the lid and allow to stand for 15 minutes.

6. Remove the foil that holds the strata using oven mitts. Move the dish to a serving dish and serve with a favorite salad.

Nutrition: Calories 191 Carbs 20g Protein 14g Fat 5g

CHAPTER 2:

Mains

6.   Lamb Provençal

Preparation time: 5 minutes

Cooking time: 8 hours

Servings: 4

Ingredients:

- 2 racks lamb, approximately 2 pounds

- 1 Tablespoon olive oil

- 2 Tablespoons fresh rosemary, chopped

- 1 Tablespoon fresh thyme, chopped

- 4 garlic cloves, minced

- 1 teaspoon dry oregano

- 1 lemon, the zest

- 1 teaspoon minced fresh ginger

- 1 cup (Good) red wine

- Salt and pepper to taste

Directions:

1. Preheat the crock-pot on low. In a pan, heat 1 tablespoon olive oil. Brown the meat for 2 minutes per side. Mix remaining ingredients in a bowl.

2. Place the lamb in the crock-pot, pour remaining seasoning over meat. Cover, cook on low for 8 hours.

Nutrition:

Calories: 140

Carbs: 3g

Fat: 5g

Protein: 21g

7.   Greek Style Lamb Shanks

Preparation time: 10 minutes

Cooking time: 6 hours

Servings: 8

Ingredients:

- 3 Tablespoons butter

- 4 lamb shanks, approximately 1 pound each

- 2 Tablespoons olive oil

- 8-10 pearl onions

- 5 garlic cloves, minced

- 2 beef tomatoes, cubed

- ¼ cup green olives

- 4 bay leaves

- 1 sprig fresh rosemary

- 1 teaspoon dry thyme

- 1 teaspoon ground cumin

- 1 cup fresh spinach

- ¾ cup hot water

- ½ cup red wine, Merlot or Cabernet

- Salt and pepper to taste

Directions:

1. In a pan, melt the butter, brown the shanks on each side. Remove from pan, add oil, onions, garlic. Cook for 3-4 minutes. Add tomatoes, olives, spices. Stir well.

2. Add liquids and return the meat. Bring to boil for 1 minute. Transfer everything to the crock-pot. Cover, cook on medium-high for 6 hours.

Nutrition:Calories: 250 Carbs: 3g Fat: 16g Protein: 22g

8. Homemade Meatballs and Spaghetti Squash

Preparation time: 15 minutes

Cooking time: 8 hours

Servings: 8

Ingredients:

- 1 medium-sized spaghetti squash, washed

- 1 Tablespoon butter, to grease crock-pot

- 2 pounds lean ground beef

- 2 garlic cloves

- 1 red onion, chopped

- ½ cup almond flour

- 2 Tablespoons of dry Parmesan cheese

- 1 egg, beaten

- 1 teaspoon ground cumin

- Salt and pepper to taste

- 4 cans diced Italian tomatoes

- 1 small can tomato paste, 28 Fl ounces

- 1 cup hot water

- 1 red onion, chopped

- ¼ cup chopped parsley

- ½ teaspoon each, salt and sugar (optional)

- 1 bay leaf

Directions:

1. Cut the spaghetti squash in half, scoop out seeds with a spoon. Grease the crock-pot, place both halves open side down in crock-pot. Mix meatball ingredients in a bowl. Form approximately 20 small meatballs.

2. In a pan, heat the olive oil. Brown the meatballs for 2-3 minutes on each side. Transfer to the crock-pot.

3. In the small bowl, add the tomatoes, tomato paste, oil, water, onion and parsley, add ½ teaspoon each of salt and sugar. Mix well.

4. Pour the marinara sauce in the crock-pot around the squash halves. Cover, cook on low for 8 hours.

Nutrition:

Calories: 409

Carbs: 31g

Fat: 18g

Protein: 32g

9.   Beef and Cabbage Roast

Preparation time: 15 minutes

Cooking time: 8 hours

Servings: 10

Ingredients:

- 1 red onion, quartered

- 2 garlic cloves, minced

- 2-3 stocks celery, diced (approximately 1 cup)

- 4-6 dry pimento berries

- 2 bay leaves

    o   pounds beef brisket (two pieces)

- 1 teaspoon chili powder

- 1 teaspoon ground cumin

- 2 cups broth, beef + 2 cups hot water

- Salt and pepper to taste

- 1 medium cabbage (approximately 2.2 pounds), cut in half, then quartered

Directions:

1. Add all ingredients, except cabbage, to crock-pot in order of list. Cover, cook on low for 7 hours. Uncover, add the cabbage on top of the stew. Re-cover, cook for 1 additional hour.

Nutrition:

Calories: 306

Carbs: 7g

Fat: 21g

Protein: 22g

CHAPTER 3:

Sides

10.   Tarragon Sweet Potatoes

Preparation time: 15 minutes

Cooking time: 3 Hours

Servings: 4

Ingredients:

- 1 pound sweet potatoes, peeled and cut into wedges

- 1 cup veggie stock

- ½ teaspoon chili powder

- ½ teaspoon cumin, ground

- Salt and black pepper to the taste

- 1 tablespoon olive oil

- 1 tablespoon tarragon, dried

- 2 tablespoons balsamic vinegar

Directions:

1. In your Crock Pot, mix the sweet potatoes with the stock, chili powder and the other Ingredients, toss, put the lid on and cook on High for 3 hours. Divide the mix between plates and serve as a side dish.

Nutrition:

Calories 80

Fat 4g

Carbs 8g

Protein 4g

11. Mint Farro Pilaf

Preparation time: 15 minutes Cooking time: 4 Hours

Servings: 2 Ingredients

- ½ tablespoon balsamic vinegar

- ½ cup whole grain farro

- A pinch of salt and black pepper

- 1 cup chicken stock

- ½ tablespoon olive oil

- 1 tablespoon green onions, chopped

- 1 tablespoon mint, chopped

Directions:

1. In your Crock Pot, mix the farro with the vinegar and the other fixings, toss, put the lid on and cook on Low for 4 hours. Divide between pates and serve.

Nutrition: Calories 162 Fat 3g Carbs 9g Protein 4g

12. Hot Zucchini Mix

Preparation time: 5 minutes

Cooking time: 2 hours

Servings: 2

Ingredients:

- ¼ cup carrots, grated

- 1-pound zucchinis, roughly cubed

- 1 teaspoon hot paprika

- ½ teaspoon chili powder

- 2 spring onions, chopped

- ½ tablespoon olive oil

- ½ teaspoon curry powder

- 1 garlic clove, minced

- ½ teaspoon ginger powder

- A pinch of salt and black pepper

- 1 tablespoon cilantro, chopped

Directions:

1. In your crock pot, mix the carrots with the zucchinis, paprika, and the rest of the fixing, toss, cook on low for 2 hours. Divide between plates and serve as a side dish.

Nutrition:

Calories: 200

Fat: 5g

Carbs: 28g

Protein: 4g

13.   Creamy Butter Parsnips

Preparation time: 15 minutes

Cooking time: 7 hours

Servings: 4

Ingredients:

- 1 cup cream

- 2 tsp butter

- 1 lb. parsnip, peeled and chopped

- 1 carrot, chopped

- 1 yellow onion, chopped

- 1 tbsp chives, chopped

- 1 tsp salt

- 1 tsp ground white pepper

- ½ tsp paprika

- 1 tbsp salt

- ¼ tsp sugar

Directions:

1. Add parsnips, carrots, and the rest of the ingredients to the crock pot. Put the crock pot's lid on and set the cooking time to 7 hours on low. Serve warm.

Nutrition:

Calories: 190

Fat: 11.2g

Carbs: 22g

Protein: 3g

14.   Butternut Squash and Eggplant Mix

Preparation time: 15 minutes

Cooking time: 4 hours

Servings: 2

Ingredients:

- 1 butternut squash, peeled and roughly cubed

- 1 eggplant, roughly cubed

- 1 red onion, chopped

- Cooking spray

- ½ cup veggie stock

- ¼ cup tomato paste

- ½ tablespoon parsley, chopped

- Salt and black pepper to the taste

- 2 garlic cloves, minced

Directions:

1. Grease the crock pot with the cooking spray and mix the squash with the eggplant, onion, and the other ingredients inside. Cook on low within 4 hours. Divide between plates and serve as a side dish. it

Nutrition:

Calories: 114

Fat: 4g

Carbs: 18g

Protein: 4g

CHAPTER 4:

Seafood

15.   Lemon-Butter Fish

Preparation time: 15 minutes

Cooking time: 5 hours

Servings: 6

Ingredients:

- 6 fillets of fresh white fish

- 2 ounces butter, soft but not melted

- 2 garlic cloves, crushed

- 1 lemon

- Handful of fresh parsley, finely chopped

Directions:

1. In a small bowl, combine the butter, garlic, zest of one lemon, chopped parsley, salt and pepper. Drizzle some olive oil into the Crock Pot.

2. Place the fish fillets into the Crock Pot and sprinkle with salt and pepper. Place a dollop of lemon butter onto each fish fillet and gently spread it out.

3. Place the lid onto the Crock Pot and set the temperature to low. Cook for 5 hours.

4. Serve each fish fillet with a generous spoonful of melted lemon butter from the bottom of the Crock Pot, and a small squeeze of lemon juice over the top!

Nutrition:

Calories: 324

Carbs: 34g

Fat: 9g

Protein: 27g

16.   Creamy Seafood Chowder

Preparation time: 15 minutes Cooking time: 5 hours

Servings: 6 Ingredients:

- 5 garlic cloves, crushed

- 1 small onion, finely chopped

- 1 cup prawns, (frozen is fine, thaw first)

- 1 cup shrimp, (frozen is fine, thaw first)

- 1 cup white fish, chopped into small chunks

- 2 cups full-fat cream

- 1 cup dry white wine

- Handful of fresh parsley, finely chopped

Directions:

1. Drizzle some olive oil into the Crock Pot. Add the garlic, onion, prawns, shrimp, white fish, cream, wine, salt, and pepper into the Crock Pot, stir to combine.

2. Place the lid onto the pot and set the temperature to low. Cook for 5 hours. Serve while hot, with a sprinkling of fresh parsley!

Nutrition:

Calories: 188

Carbs: 17g

Fat: 9g

Protein: 8g

17.   Salmon and Garlic Greens

Preparation time: 15 minutes

Cooking time: 3 hours

Servings: 4

Ingredients:

- 4 salmon fillets, skin on

- 4 garlic cloves, crushed

- ½ a head of broccoli, cut into florets

- 2 cups frozen green beans

Directions:

1. Drizzle some olive oil into the Crock Pot. Place the salmon fillets, (skin-side down) into the pot and sprinkle them with salt and pepper.

2. Place the broccoli, beans, and garlic on top of the salmon, sprinkle the veggies with salt and pepper. Drizzle some more olive oil over top of the veggies and fish.

3. Place the lid onto the pot and set the temperature to high. Cook for 3 hours. Serve immediately!

Nutrition:

Calories: 80

Carbs: 10g

Fat: 4g

Protein: 4g

18.   Prawn and Sausage Casserole

Preparation time: 15 minutes Cooking time: 6 hours

Servings: 6

Ingredients:

- 1 ½ cups frozen prawns, (thawed)

- 3 sausages, chopped into chunks

- 5 garlic cloves, crushed

- 1 small onion, finely chopped

- 4 tomatoes, chopped

- 1 tsp mixed dried herbs

- 2 tsp mixed dried spices – coriander, cumin, chili (choose your favorites)

Directions:

1. Drizzle some olive oil into the Crock Pot. Place the prawns, sausages, garlic, onion, tinned tomatoes, herbs, spices, salt, and pepper into the pot and stir to combine.

2. Place the lid onto the pot and set the temperature to low. Cook for 6 hours. Serve while hot, with a sprinkling of fresh herbs such as coriander and parsley!

Nutrition:

Calories: 401

Carbs: 9g

Fat: 13g

Protein: 42g

19.   Coconut Fish Curry

Preparation time: 15 minutes Cooking time: 4 hours

Servings: 4-6 Ingredients:

- 4 large fillets of fresh white fish, cut into chunks

- 4 garlic cloves, crushed

- 1 small onion, finely chopped

- 1 tsp ground turmeric

- 2 tbsp yellow curry paste

- 2 cups fish stock

- 2 cans full-fat coconut milk

- 1 lime Fresh coriander, roughly chopped

Directions:

1. Drizzle some olive oil into the Crock Pot. Add the garlic, onion, turmeric, curry paste, fish, stock, coconut milk, salt, and pepper to the pot, stir to combine.

2. Place the lid onto the pot and set the temperature to high. Cook for 4 hours. Serve while hot, with a small squeeze of fresh lime juice and fresh coriander!

Nutrition:

Calories: 353

Carbs: 32g

Fat: 18g

Protein: 19g

CHAPTER 5:

Poultry

20. Buffalo Chicken Lettuce Wraps

Preparation time: 10 minutes

Cooking Time: 8 hours 30 minutes

Servings: 2

Ingredients:

- 1 1/2 chicken breasts, skinless and boneless

- 1/2 celery stalk

- 8 oz chicken broth

- 1/2 cup hot wing sauce

- large lettuce leaves

Directions:

1. Combine the first three ingredients in the crockpot. Cover and cook for 8 hours on low. When cooked, remove chicken from the pot and shred with fork.

2. Return the chicken to the pot with hot wing sauce and cook on high for another 30 minutes. Serve on lettuce cups.

Nutrition:

Calories: 312

Fat: 24 g

Carbs: 3.9 g

Protein: 34 g

21.   Green Chili Chicken

Preparation time: 10 minutes

Cooking Time: 6 hours 30 minutes

Servings: 2

Ingredients:

- 2 chicken thighs, thawed

- 2 oz green chili

- 1 tsp garlic salt

Directions:

1. Place chicken in the crockpot and cook for 6 hours on low. Drain the juices afterwards and add in the other two ingredients.

2. Cover and cook for another 30 minutes on high. Shred chicken with a fork.

Nutrition: Calories: 347 Fat: 23.8 g Carbs: 3.7 g Protein: 33.1 g

22.   Italian Buffalo Chicken

Preparation time: 5 minutes

Cooking Time: 6 hours

Servings: 2

Ingredients:

- 2 chicken breasts, boneless and skinless

- 1/2 cup buffalo wing sauce

- 1/2 cup Italian dressing

Directions:

1. Put all ingredients in the crockpot. Mix thoroughly. Cook on low for 6 hours.

Nutrition: Calories: 287 Fat: 17 g Carbs: 3 g Protein: 29 g

23.   Chicken Picatta

Preparation time: 10 minutes

Cooking Time: 3 hours

Servings: 2

Ingredients:

- 2 chicken breasts

- 1/4 cup tomatoes, diced

- 2 tbsp melted butter

- 7 oz artichoke hearts, quartered

Directions:

1. Except for the parmesan, combine all ingredients in the crockpot, including garlic cloves and pepper to taste. Cook on high for 3 hours. Top with parmesan cheese.

Nutrition: Calories: 343 Fat: 29 g Carbs: 6 g Protein: 37 g

24. Lemon Garlic Chicken

Preparation time: 15 minutes

Cooking time: 3-4 hours

Servings: 6

Ingredients:

- 1 cup vegetable broth

- 1½ teaspoons grated lemon peel

- 3 tablespoons lemon juice

- 2 tablespoons capers, drained

- 3 garlic cloves, minced

- ½ teaspoon pepper

- 6 boneless skinless chicken breast halves (6 ounces / 170 g each)

- 2 tablespoons butter

- 2 tablespoons all-purpose flour

- ½ cup heavy whipping cream

- Hot cooked rice

Directions:

1. In a small bowl, combine the first six ingredients. Place chicken in a crock pot; pour broth mixture over chicken. Cook, covered, on low 3 to 4 hours or until chicken is tender. Remove chicken from crock pot; keep warm.

2. In a large saucepan, melt butter over medium heat. Stir in flour until smooth; gradually whisk in cooking juices.

3. Bring to a boil, stirring constantly; cook and stir 1-2 minutes or until thickened. Remove from heat and stir in cream. Serve chicken and rice with sauce.

Nutrition:

Calories: 265

Carbs: 25g

Fat: 3g

Protein: 34g

CHAPTER 6:

Meat

25.   Unspicy Beef Chili

Preparation time: 15 minutes

Cooking time: 8 hours

Servings: 8

Ingredients:

- 2 cans diced tomatoes

- 2 tablespoons smoked paprika

- 1 pound ground beef

- 1 onion, chopped

- 1 green bell pepper, chopped

- 8 ounces of Portobello mushrooms, sliced

- 2 cloves of garlic, minced

- 1 tablespoon butter

- salt and pepper to taste

Directions:

1. Turn on the crockpot and set to high cooking setting. Add the tomatoes and paprika and stir. Stir in the ground beef and sauté for 3 minutes.

2. Add the rest of the ingredients. Change the heat setting to low and cook for 8 hours.

Nutrition:

Calories: 188

Carbohydrates: 6.42g

Protein: 16.3g

Fat: 11.15g

26.   Island Lamb Stew

Preparation time: 15 minutes Cooking time: 8 hours

Servings: 4 Ingredients:

- 1 tablespoon butter

- 1 cup onion, sliced

- 1 pound lamb, diced

- 1 cup celery, sliced

- ¾ cup green pepper, chopped

- 1 tablespoon curry powder

- 1 can tomatoes

- salt and pepper to taste

Directions:

1. Set the crockpot to high heat and add butter. Sauté the onions

   for a minute then add the lamb. Sear the lamb for 3 minutes.

2. Pour the remaining ingredients. Close the lid and set the heat to low. Cook for 8 hours.

Nutrition:

Calories: 352

Carbohydrates: 7.83g

Protein: 29.32g

Fat: 22.4 g

27.   Steak Pizzaiola

Preparation time: 15 minutes

Cooking time: 8 hours & 20 minutes

Servings: 4

Ingredients:

- 12 oz flank steak

- 1 sweet bell pepper, de-seeded and sliced

- 2 tablespoons Italian seasoning

- 12 oz pasta sauce, sugar-free

- 4 oz shredded mozzarella cheese

Directions:

1. Grease a 4-quart crock pot with a non-stick cooking spray. Season the beef with salt, ground black pepper, and Italian seasoning, place in the crock pot, then pour in the pasta sauce.

2. Top with peppers and cover the crock pot with its lid. Set the cooking timer for 6 to 8 hours, and allow to cook at a low heat setting.

3. Remove the beef, and keep warm. Add the mozzarella to the crock pot, allowing to melt, but cooking for a further 20 minutes. To serve, slice the beef, and serve alongside the tomato mixture.

Nutrition:

Calories: 211

Carbohydrates: 4 g

Fats: 9.4 g

Protein: 26.3 g

28.   Sweet and Spicy Meatballs

Preparation time: 15 minutes Cooking time: 8 hours

Servings: 4

Ingredients:

- 12 oz meatballs

- 14 oz chili sauce, sugar-free

- 12 oz raspberry jam, sugar-free

Directions:

1. Grease a 4-quart crock pot with a non-stick cooking spray, and place the meatballs inside. Stir the chili sauce and the jam together in a bowl, then add to the crock pot.

2. Cover the crock pot with its lid, and set the cooking timer for 8 hours, allowing to cook at a low heat setting. Serve with cauliflower rice.

Nutrition: Calories: 92 Carbohydrates: 4.5 g Carbs: 3.9 g Fats: 5.1 g

Protein: 7 g

29.   Beef Ragu

Preparation time: 15 minutes

Cooking time: 8 hours & 5 minutes

Servings: 8

Ingredients:

- 12 oz beef short ribs, trimmed and cut into chunks

- 1 cup white onion, peeled and sliced

- 4 cups chopped tomatoes

- 3 tablespoons tomato paste, sugar-free

- 1 teaspoon dried basil and dried oregano

Directions:

1. Season the beef with salt and ground black pepper. Place a large skillet over a medium heat, add a tablespoon of olive oil, then add the beef pieces.

2. Allow to cook for 4 to 5 minutes, turning until all sides are seared. Grease a 4-quart crock pot with a non-stick cooking spray and add the remaining ingredients, mixing well.

3. Add the seared beef pieces, and place the lid on the crock pot. Allow to cook for 6 to 8 hours at a low heat setting.

4. Shred the beef with forks, and return it to the cooking liquid. Allow it to sit for 15 minutes. Garnish with grated cheese, and serve with zucchini noodles.

Nutrition:

Calories: 513.4

Carbohydrates: 12.4 g

Fats: 29.7 g

Protein: 45.8 g

CHAPTER 7:

Vegetables

30.   Aubergine & Tomato Platter

Preparation time: 15 minutes

Cooking time: 6-8 hours

Servings: 6

Ingredients:

- 4 tbsps. olive oil

- 17½ sliced aubergines

- 2 crushed garlic cloves

- 1 sliced red onion

- 10½ oz. quartered tomatoes

- 1¾ oz. sundried tomatoes

- 1 sliced fennel bulb

- 1 tsp. coriander seeds

- Salt

- Pepper

- 3 1/2 oz. feta cheese

- 1¾ oz. toasted flaked almonds

Sauce:

- 1 bunch chopped parsley 1 bunch chopped basil

- 1 bunch chopped chives 2 tbsps. olive oil

- 2 tsps. capers 1 squeezed lemon juice

Directions:

1. Pour 2 tbsps. olive oil in a crock pot along with the onions and garlic. Brush the aubergines with the rest of the oil and spread them in the crock pot.

2. Spread the fennel and tomatoes over the aubergines and sprinkle salt, pepper and coriander seeds on top. Add the remaining ingredients in a bowl and pour it over the corn. Cook covered for 6-8 hours on low.

3. Using a food processor, place the sauce ingredients and process until smooth. Transfer the crock pot contents onto a platter and sprinkle the sauce over it.

4. Serve garnished with almonds and feta cheese.

Nutrition:

Calories: 269

Fat: 20 g

Carbs: 11 g

Protein: 8 g

31. Pesto Mushrooms with Ricotta

Preparation time: 15 minutesCooking time: 8-9 hours

Servings: 4 Ingredients:

- 5 tbsps. virgin olive oil

- 16 chestnut mushrooms

- 8¾ oz. ricotta

- 2 chopped garlic cloves

- 2 tbsps. green pesto

- 24g grated Parmesan

- 2 tbsps. chopped parsley

- Extra Pesto

Directions:

1. Brush the mushrooms with oil and place in a crock pot cap side down, in a single layer. Mix together the rest of the ingredients except the oil and Parmesan.

2. Spoon the mixture into the mushrooms. Sprinkle the Parmesan and remaining oil over. Cook for 8-9 hours on low. Serve with extra pesto.

Nutrition:

Calories: 400

Fat: 34 g

Carbs: 2 g

Protein: 19 g

32.   Creamy Spinach Curry

Preparation time: 15 minutesCooking time: 3-4 hours

Servings: 8

Ingredients:

- 10 oz. frozen spinach

- 1 chopped onion

- 4 minced garlic cloves

- 2 tbsps. curry powder

- 2 tbsps. melted butter

- ½ cup vegetable stock

- ¼ cup heavy cream

- 1 tsp. lemon juice

Directions:

1. Dump all ingredients in a crock pot except the cream and lemon

    juice. Cook covered for 3-4 hours on low.

2. Mix in the lemon juice and cream, 30 minutes prior to the completion of cook time and cook covered.

Nutrition:

Calories: 91

Fat: 6 g

Carbs: 3 g

Protein: 4 g

33. Coconut Sauced Kale & Squash

Preparation time: 15 minutes

Cooking time: 4 hours

Servings: 5

Ingredients:

- 1 chopped butternut squash

- 1 bunch chopped Kale

- Salt

- 1 tsp. chili flakes

- 14 oz. coconut milk

- ¾ cup water

- ½ chopped onion

- 1 tbsp. coconut aminos

Directions:

1. Dump all ingredients in a crock pot. Cook covered for 4 hours on low, stirring in between. Stir mix and serve.

Nutrition:

Calories: 271

Fat: 22 g

Carbs: 20 g

Protein: 5 g

34.   Tomato Soup

Preparation time: 15 minutes

Cooking time: 4 hours

Servings: 4

Ingredients:

- 1 can crushed tomatoes

- 1 cup vegetable broth

- ½ cup heavy cream

- 2 tablespoons chopped parsley

- ½ teaspoon onion powder

- ½ teaspoon garlic powder

- Salt and pepper to taste

Directions:

1. Put all the fixings except heavy cream in the crockpot, then cook on low for 4 hours. Blend then stir in the cream using an

immersion blender. Taste and season with more salt and pepper if necessary.

Nutrition:

Calories: 90

Carbs: 20g

Fat: 0g

Protein: 2g

35.   Vegetable Korma

Preparation time: 15 minutesCooking time: 8 hours

Servings: 4 Ingredients:

- 1 head's worth of cauliflower florets
- ¾ can of full-fat coconut milk
- 2 cups chopped green beans
- ½ chopped onion 2 minced garlic cloves
- 2 tablespoons curry powder
- 2 tablespoons coconut flour
- 1 teaspoon garam masala
- Salt and pepper to taste

Directions:

1. Add vegetables into your crockpot. Mix coconut milk with seasonings. Pour into the crockpot. Sprinkle over coconut flour and mix until blended.

2. Close and cook on low for 8 hours. Taste and season more if necessary. Serve!

Nutrition:

Calories: 310

Carbs: 41g

Fat: 12g

Protein: 9g

36. Zoodles with Cauliflower-Tomato Sauce

Preparation time: 15 minutesCooking time: 3 hours & 31 minutes

Servings: 4 Ingredients:

- 5 large spiralized zucchinis

- 2 24-ounce cans of diced tomatoes

- 2 small heads' worth of cauliflower florets

- 1 cup chopped sweet onion

- 4 minced garlic cloves

- ½ cup veggie broth 5 teaspoons Italian seasoning

- Salt and pepper to taste

- Enough water to cover zoodles

Directions:

1. Put everything but the zoodles into your crockpot. Cook on high for 3 ½ hours. Smash into a chunky sauce with a potato masher or another utensil.

2. To cook the zoodles, boil a large pot of water. When boiling, cook zoodles for just 1 minute, then drain—Season with salt and pepper. Serve sauce over zoodles!

Nutrition:

Calories: 170

Carbs: 22g

Fat: 6g

Protein: 11g

CHAPTER 8:

Soups & Stews

37.   Cretan Beef Stew

Preparation Time: 15 minutes

Cooking Time: 6 hours

Servings: 6

Ingredients:

- 2 lb. lean beef, cut into bite-sized cubes

- 2 onions, chopped

- 1 lb. eggplant, cubed

- 1 lb. zucchini, sliced

- 1 lb. tomatoes, chopped

- 1 tsp. dried thyme

- 2 tbsp. fresh mint, chopped

- Salt and freshly ground black pepper, to taste

- 5 tbsp. extra-virgin olive oil

- 5 cups water

Directions:

1. In a crock pot, place all the ingredients and stir to combine. Set the crock pot on "High" and cook, covered for about 6 hours. Serve hot.

Nutrition:

Calories: 441

Carbohydrates: 13.6g

Protein: 48.7g

Fat: 21.6g

38.   Winter Dinner Lamb Stew

Preparation Time: 15 minutes

Cooking Time: 3¼ hours

Servings: 8

Ingredients:

- 8 lamb shoulder chops

- Salt and freshly ground black pepper, to taste

- 3 tbsp. olive oil

- 8 garlic cloves, chopped

- 1 large onion, chopped

- 4 large plum tomatoes, chopped

- 2 cups chicken broth

- 1½ cups water

- 1½ lb. fresh chicory, chopped roughly

- ¼ cup fresh lemon juice

- ½ cup fresh dill, chopped

Directions:

1. Season the lamb chops with salt and black pepper evenly. In a large skillet, heat 2 tbsp. of the oil over medium-high heat and sea the chops in 2 batches for about 3 minutes per side

2. With a slotted spoon, transfer the chops into a crock pot. In the same skillet, heat the remaining oil over medium heat and sauté the onion and garlic for about 5-6 minutes.

3. Add the tomatoes and cook for about 2-3 minutes, stirring frequently. Add the broth and bring to a boil, scraping up the browned bits from the bottom.

4. Remove from the heat and transfer the mixture to the crock pot. Add the water and stir to combine. Set the crock pot on "High" and cook, covered for about 2 hours.

5. Uncover the crock pot and spread the chicory on the top of the stew. Set the crock pot on "High" and cook, covered for about 1 hour, stirring 2-3 times.

6. Uncover the crock pot and stir in the lemon juice and dill. Serve hot.

Nutrition:

Calories: 500

Carbohydrates: 12.5g

Protein: 55.5g

Fat: 26.7g

39.　Middle Eastern Comforting Stew

Preparation Time: 20 minutes

Cooking Time: 6¼ hours

Servings: 6

Ingredients:

- 2½ lb. lamb shoulder chops, cut into 1-inch cubes

- ½ tsp. dried mint

- 2 tsp. ground coriander

- 1 tsp. ground cumin

- ¼ tsp. ground turmeric

- ¼ tsp. red chili powder

- Salt and freshly ground black pepper, to taste

- 2 tbsp. olive oil, divided

- 1 medium onion, chopped

- 4 garlic cloves, minced

- 1 tbsp. fresh ginger, minced

- 1½ cup chicken broth

- 3 cups tomato sauce

- ½ cup tomatoes, chopped

- 1 (15-oz.) can chickpeas, drained and rinsed

- 2 cups baby potatoes, halved

- 1 cup fresh spinach, chopped

Directions:

1. In a large bowl, add the lamb cubes, dried mint and spices and toss to coat well. In a large skillet, heat 1 tbsp. of the oil over medium heat and sear the lamb cubes for about 6 minutes or until browned completely.

2. With a slotted spoon, transfer the lamb cubes into a crock pot. In the same skillet, heat the remaining oil over medium heat and sauté the onion, garlic and ginger for about 5-6 minutes.

3. Add the broth and tomato sauce and bring to a boil.

4. Transfer the onion mixture into the crock pot with tomatoes, chickpeas and potatoes and stir to combine. Set the crock pot on "Low" and cook, covered for about 6 hours.

5. Uncover the crock pot and stir in the spinach until wilted. Serve hot.

Nutrition:

Calories: 675

Carbohydrates: 61.7g

Protein: 54.9g

Fat: 24.9g

40.   Richly Flavored Lamb Stew

Preparation Time: 15 minutes

Cooking Time: 8 hours 50 minutes

Servings: 6

Ingredients:

- 2 tbsp. olive oil

- 2¼ lb. lamb shoulder, cubed

- 2 onions, sliced

- 5 garlic cloves, crushed

- 1 tsp. fresh ginger, grated

- 1 tbsp. ground cumin

- 1 tbsp. ground coriander

- 1 tsp. ground cinnamon

- Pinch of saffron

- 1 tsp. lemon peel, grated

- 1 tbsp. tomato puree

- 2 ½ cups hot beef broth

- Salt and freshly ground black pepper, to taste

- 1 cup Kalamata olives, pitted

- 1 tbsp. honey

- 2 tbsp. fresh lemon juice

Directions:

1. In a large skillet, heat 1 tbsp. of the 4-5 minutes or until browned completely. With a slotted spoon, transfer the lamb cubes into a crock pot.

2. In the same skillet, heat the remaining oil over medium heat and sauté the onion for about 4-6 minutes. Add the garlic and ginger and sauté for about 1-2 minutes.

3. Add the spices, saffron, lemon peel and tomato puree and sauté for about 1-2 minutes. Transfer the onion mixture into the crock pot with broth, salt and black pepper and stir to combine.

4. Set the crock pot on "Low" and cook, covered for about 6-8 hours. Uncover the crock pot and stir in the olives, honey and lemon juice.

5. Set the crock pot on "High" and cook, covered for about 20-30 minutes. Serve hot.

Nutrition:

Calories: 435

Carbohydrates: 10.3g

Protein: 50.9g

Fat: 2-.4g

41.   Pork Stew

Preparation Time: 15 minutes

Cooking Time: 10 hours

Servings: 6

Ingredients:

- 2 lb. boneless pork loin, cut into 1-inch pieces

- 1/3 cup all-purpose flour

- ½ tsp. dried thyme

- ½ tsp. ground cinnamon

- 1 (14½-oz.) can chicken broth

- ¾ cups dry red wine

- 1 tbsp. balsamic vinegar

- 1 tbsp. honey

- 2 cups frozen pearl onions

- 4 oz. feta cheese, crumbled

Directions:

1. In a bowl, add the pork cubes, flour, thyme and cinnamon and toss to coat well. In a bowl, add broth, wine, vinegar and honey and beat until well combined.

2. In the bottom of a crock pot, place the pork cubes and onions and top with broth mixture. Set the crock pot on "Low" and cook, covered for about 9-10 hours. Serve hot with the topping of feta cheese.

Nutrition:

Calories: 354

Carbohydrates: 13.8g

Protein: 44.8g

Fat: 9.8g

CHAPTER 9:

Snacks

42.   Eggplant and Tomato Salsa

Preparation Time: 10 minutes

Cooking Time: 7 hours

Servings: 4

Ingredients:

- 1 ½ cup chopped tomatoes

- 3 cups cubed eggplant

- 2 tsps. capers

- 6 oz. sliced green olives

- 4 minced garlic cloves

- 2 tsps. balsamic vinegar

- 1 tbsp. chopped basil

- Salt

- Black pepper

Directions:

1. In your crock pot, mix tomatoes with eggplant, capers, green olives, garlic, vinegar, basil, salt and pepper, toss, cover and cook on Low for 7 hours. Divide salsa into small bowls and serve.

Nutrition:

Calories: 200

Fat: 6 g

Carbs: 9 g

Protein: 2 g

43. Carrots and Cauliflower Spread

Preparation Time: 10 mins

Cooking Time: 7 hours

Servings: 4

Ingredients:

- 1 cup sliced carrots

- 1½ cup cauliflower florets

- 1/3 cup cashews

- ½ cup chopped turnips

- 2½ cups water

- 1 cup coconut milk

- 1 tsp. garlic powder

- ¼ cup nutritional yeast

- ¼ tsp. smoked paprika

- ¼ tsp. mustard powder

- Salt

- Black pepper

Directions:

1. In your crock pot, mix carrots with cauliflower, cashews, turnips and water, stir, cover and cook on Low for 7 hours.

2. Drain, transfer to a blender, add milk, garlic powder, yeast, paprika, mustard powder, salt and pepper, blend well, divide into bowls and serve as a party spread. Enjoy!

Nutrition:

Calories: 291

Fat: 7 g

Carbs: 14 g

Protein: 3 g

44.   Pizza

Preparation Time: 10 minutes

Cooking Time: 3 hours

Servings: 4

Ingredients:

- ½ pound Ground pork

- 1 tbsp Pizza seasoning

- ½ can Tomatoes

- 1 cup Mozzarella

- ½ pound Ground beef

- ½ cup Peppers

- ½ cup Black olives

- ½ jar Low carb pizza sauce

- ½ cup Onions

- 15 Pepperoni slices

- ½ cup Mushrooms

Directions:

1. Brown both the meats. Add them to the crock pot. Add spices, mushrooms and vegetables. Pour in the sauce and tomatoes.

2. Evenly distribute cheese. Add pepperoni. Cook on low for 3 hours.

Nutrition:

Calories: 441

Fat: 30g

Carb: 6g

Protein: 33g

45.   Bacon Chicken Chowder

Preparation Time: 10 minutes

Cooking Time: 8 hours

Servings: 4

Ingredients:

- 2 cloves Garlic

- 1 Leek

- 3 oz Mushrooms

- 2 tbsp Butter

- ½ pound Chicken

- ½ cup Heavy cream

- ½ tsp Salt

- ½ tsp Garlic powder

- 1 Shallot

- 1 rib Celery

- ½ Sweet onion

- 1 cup Chicken stock

- 4 oz Cream cheese

- ½ pound Bacon

- ½ tsp Black pepper

- ½ tsp Thyme, dried

Directions:

1. Chop the onion, celery, shallot, bacon, chicken, mushrooms, leek, and dice the garlic. Cook the chicken until done.

2. Add all the ingredients to the crock pot. Stir everything well. Cook on low for 8 hours.

Nutrition:

Calories: 355

Fat: 28g

Carb: 6.4g

Protein: 21g

46.   Glazed Walnuts

Preparation Time: 10 minutes

Cooking Time: 2 hours

Servings: 8

Ingredients:

- 8 oz Walnuts

- ¼ cup Keto sweetener

- ¼ cup Butter

- ½ tsp Vanilla extract

Directions:

1. Put all ingredients in the crock pot. Cook on low for 2 hours. Cool and serve.

Nutrition: Calories: 264 Fat: 24g Carb: 8g Protein: 4g

CHAPTER 10:

Desserts

47.   Apple Cherry Cobbler

Preparation time: 15 minutes

Cooking time: 4 hours

Servings: 10

Ingredients:

- 1 pound cherries, pitted

- 4 red apples, peeled and sliced

- 4 tablespoons maple syrup

- 2 tablespoons cornstarch

- 1 tablespoon lemon juice

- 1 1/4 cups all-purpose flour

- 1/2 cup butter, chilled and cubed

- 2 tablespoons white sugar

- 1/2 cup buttermilk, chilled

Directions:

1. Combine the cherries, apples, maple syrup, cornstarch and lemon juice in your crock pot. For the topping, mix the flour, butter and sugar in a bowl and rub the mix well with your fingertips until grainy.

2. Stir in the buttermilk and give it a quick mix. Spoon the batter over the fruit mixture and bake on low settings for 4 hours. Serve the cobbler chilled.

Nutrition:

Calories: 330

Carbs: 57g

Fat: 10g Protein: 2g

48. Nutty Pear Streusel Dessert

Preparation time: 15 minutesCooking time: 4 hours

Servings: 4 Ingredients:

- 4 large apples, peeled and cubed

- 1/2 cup golden raisins

- 1 teaspoon cinnamon powder

- 1/2 cup pecans, chopped

- 1 cup ground almonds

- 2 tablespoons all-purpose flour

- 2 tablespoons melted butter

- 2 tablespoons brown sugar1 pinch salt

Directions:

1. Mix the apples, raisins and cinnamon in your crock pot. For the topping, combine the pecans, almonds, flour, melted butter, sugar and salt and rub the mix well with your fingertips.

2. Spread this mixture over the pears and cook for 4 hours on low settings. This dessert is best served chilled.

Nutrition:

Calories: 150

Carbs: 27g

Fat: 6g

Protein: 3g

49. Pumpkin Croissant Pudding

Preparation time: 15 minutes

Cooking time: 5 hours

Servings: 6

Ingredients:

- 6 large croissants, cubed

- 1 cup skim milk

- 1 1/2 cups pumpkin puree

- 3 eggs

- 1 teaspoon cinnamon powder

- 1/4 cup white sugar

Directions:

1. Place the croissants in your crock pot. Mix the milk, pumpkin puree, eggs, cinnamon and sugar in a bowl. Pour this mixture over the croissants.

2. Cover the pot with its lid and cook on low settings for 5 hours.

   Serve the pudding chilled.

Nutrition:

Calories: 363

Carbs: 47g

Fat: 16g

Protein: 6g

50.   Strawberry Fudgy Brownies

Preparation time: 15 minutes

Cooking time: 2 hours

Servings: 8

Ingredients:

- 1/2 cup butter, cubed

- 1 cup dark chocolate chips

- 2 eggs

- 1/2 cup white sugar

- 1/2 cup applesauce˙

- 1/4 cup cocoa powder

- 1/2 cup all-purpose flour

- 1 pinch salt

- 1 1/2 cups fresh strawberries, halved

Directions:

1. Mix the butter and chocolate in a bowl and place over a hot water bath to melt until smooth. Remove from heat and add the eggs, sugar and applesauce and give it a good mix.

2. Fold in the cocoa powder, flour and salt and pour the mixture in your crock pot. Top with strawberries and cook on high settings for 2 hours. Allow to cool before cutting into cubes and serving.

Nutrition:

Calories: 168

Carbs: 21g

Fat: 9g

Protein: 2g

Conclusion

You have to the end of this amazing cookbook, but always remember that this is not the end of your cooking journey with the crockpot; but instead, this is your stepping stone towards more cooking glory. We hope you have found your favorite recipes that are time-saving and money-saving.

Now that you know how Crockpot works and the many benefits of using it, maybe it is time for you to buy one for your family, in case you haven't owned one. When it comes to time spent preparing meals for your family, Crock-Pot is a lifesaver. If you are a busy person, a powerful solution is to use the crockpot.

You will also love to own one if you want to make your life simpler at work if you want to make your life simpler at home, and if you want to preserve some of the natural resources. You could also use one if you want to lean towards a healthier lifestyle as cooking in the crockpot is conducive to health than in the oven.

The crockpot can be used in making homemade and custom-made buffets, even in catering services. You can use it for cooking for your staff for special occasions and for showing them how to cook a tasty and healthier dish for your guests well within their own crockpot.

After choosing the best one for you, maybe it is time for you to know more about the recipes you should use. There are various recipes in this cookbook that are perfect for crockpot cooking, and they will definitely be useful and beneficial for you.

Moreover, whether you are a newbie or an experienced cook, you are going to love this cookbook as it is packed with every conceivable taste. You have discovered more than 1000 recipes in this cookbook that you can put into practice using your crockpot. You can always customize the recipes to suit your taste buds, as you can make any recipe mild or hot, sweet or sour; you have all the freedom to make the recipes your own. The best thing about cooking using a crockpot is that you just need to add the main ingredients, and no other complicated cooking preparation is needed; the crockpot will add most of the other ingredients for you.

CPSIA information can be obtained
at www.ICGtesting.com
Printed in the USA
BVHW010809270421
605885BV00018B/152